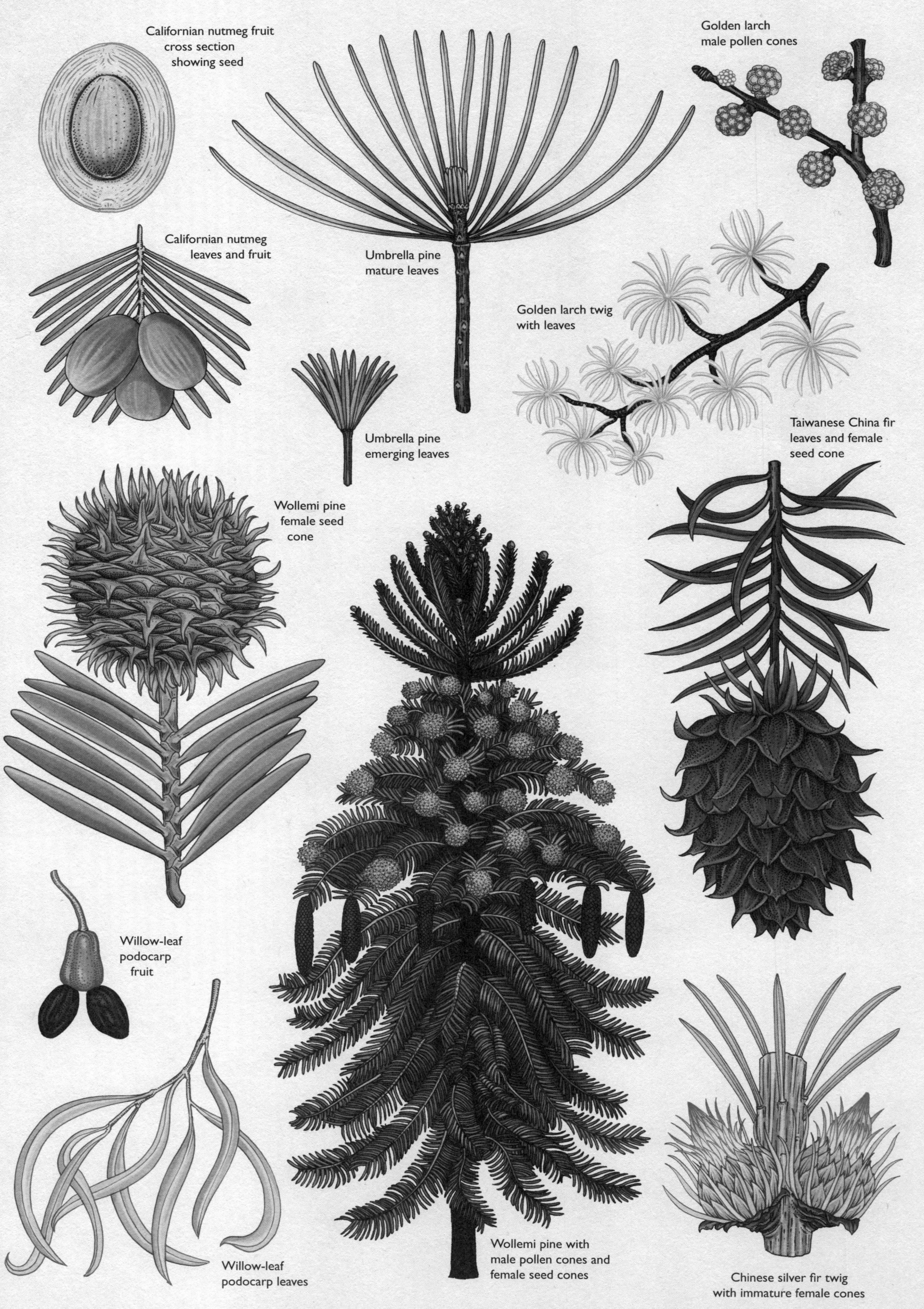

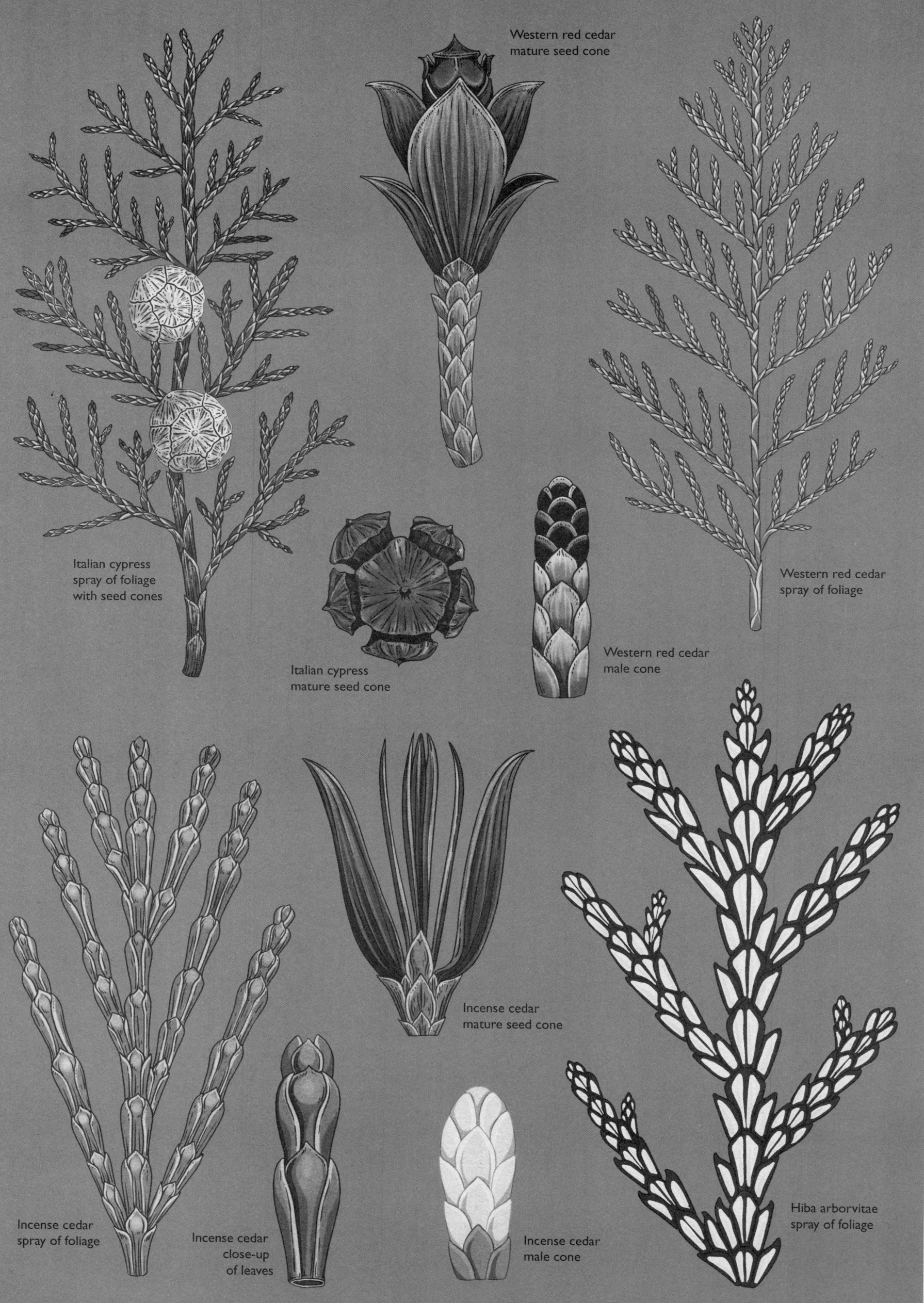

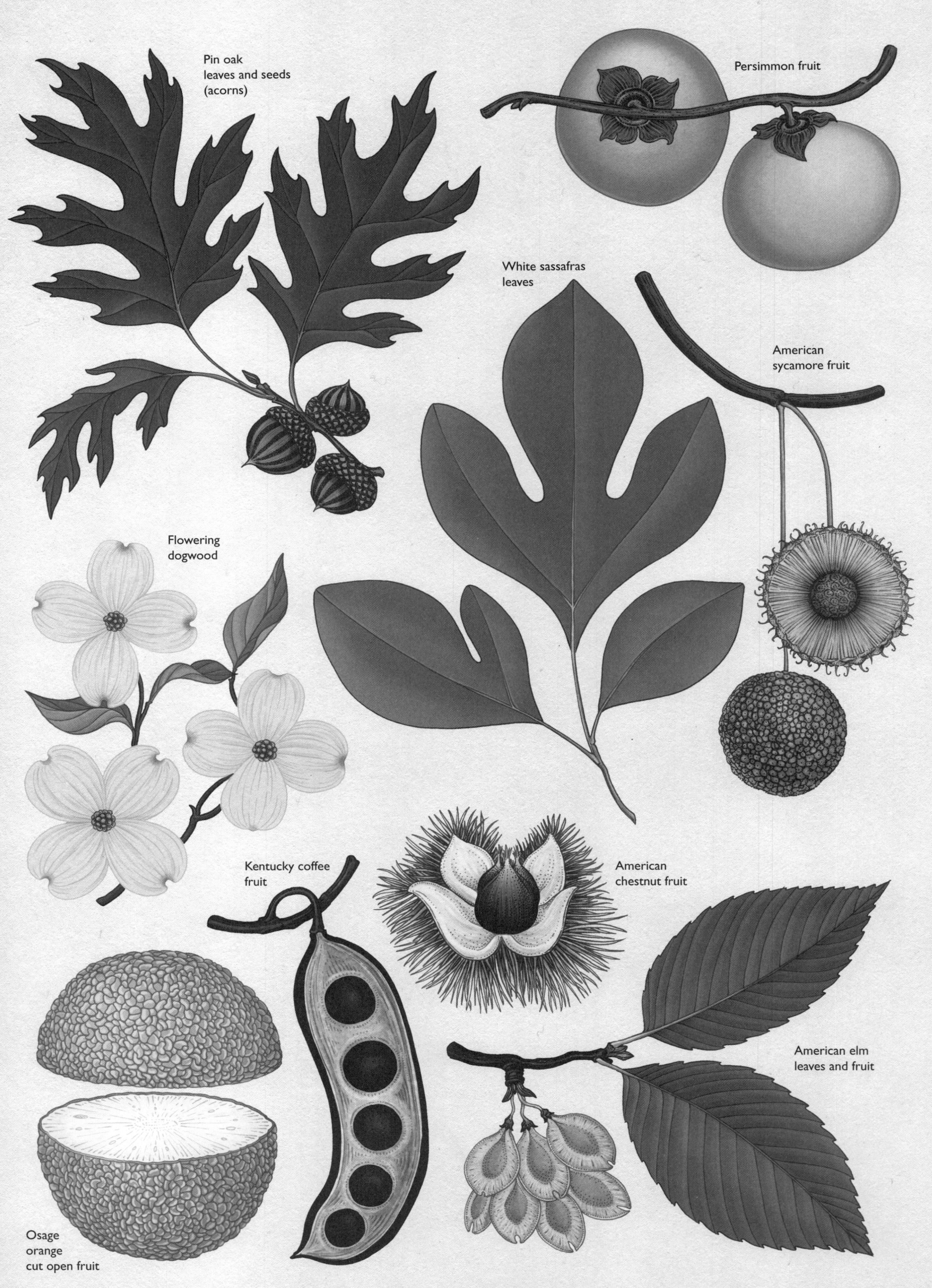

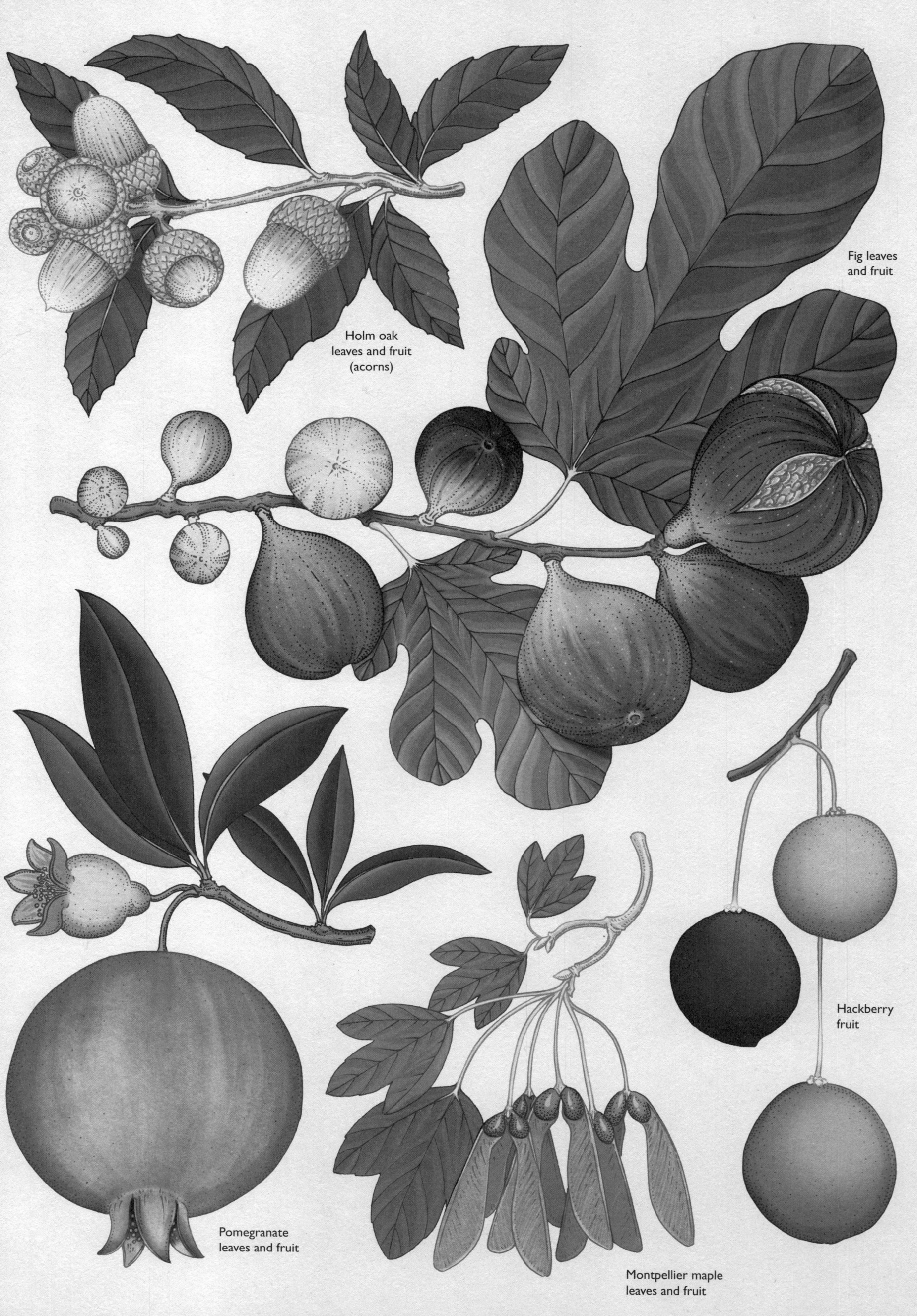

Red mallee young seed pods

Bell-fruited mallee flower

Red mallee leaves and flowers

Soap mallee leaves

Red-flowered mallee flower

Red-flowered mallee flower bud

Mallee wattle leaves

Soap mallee flower

Red-flowered mallee breaking bud

Soap mallee fruit

Mallee wattle flower buds

Mallee wattle flowers

Western black tea flowers

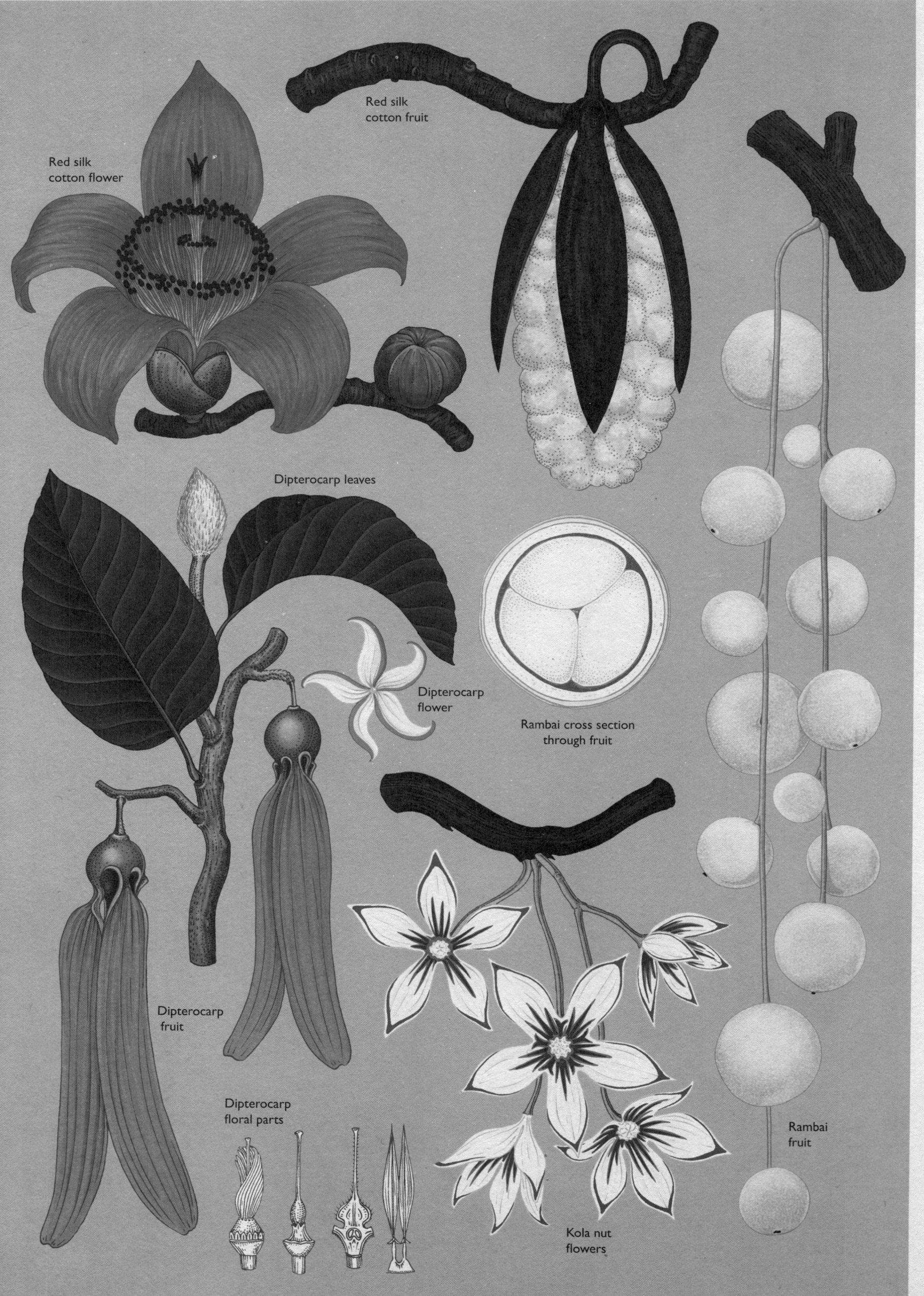

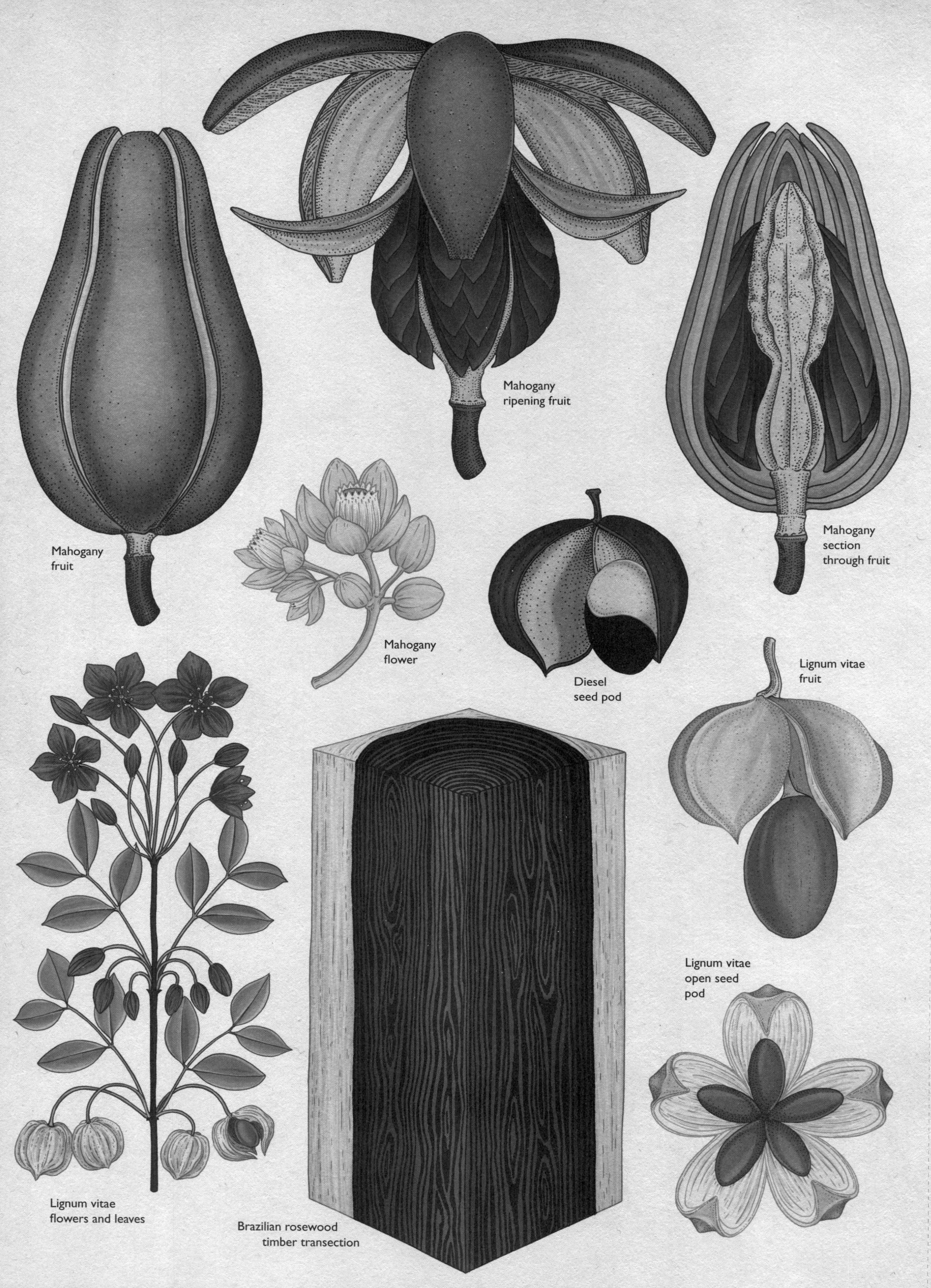

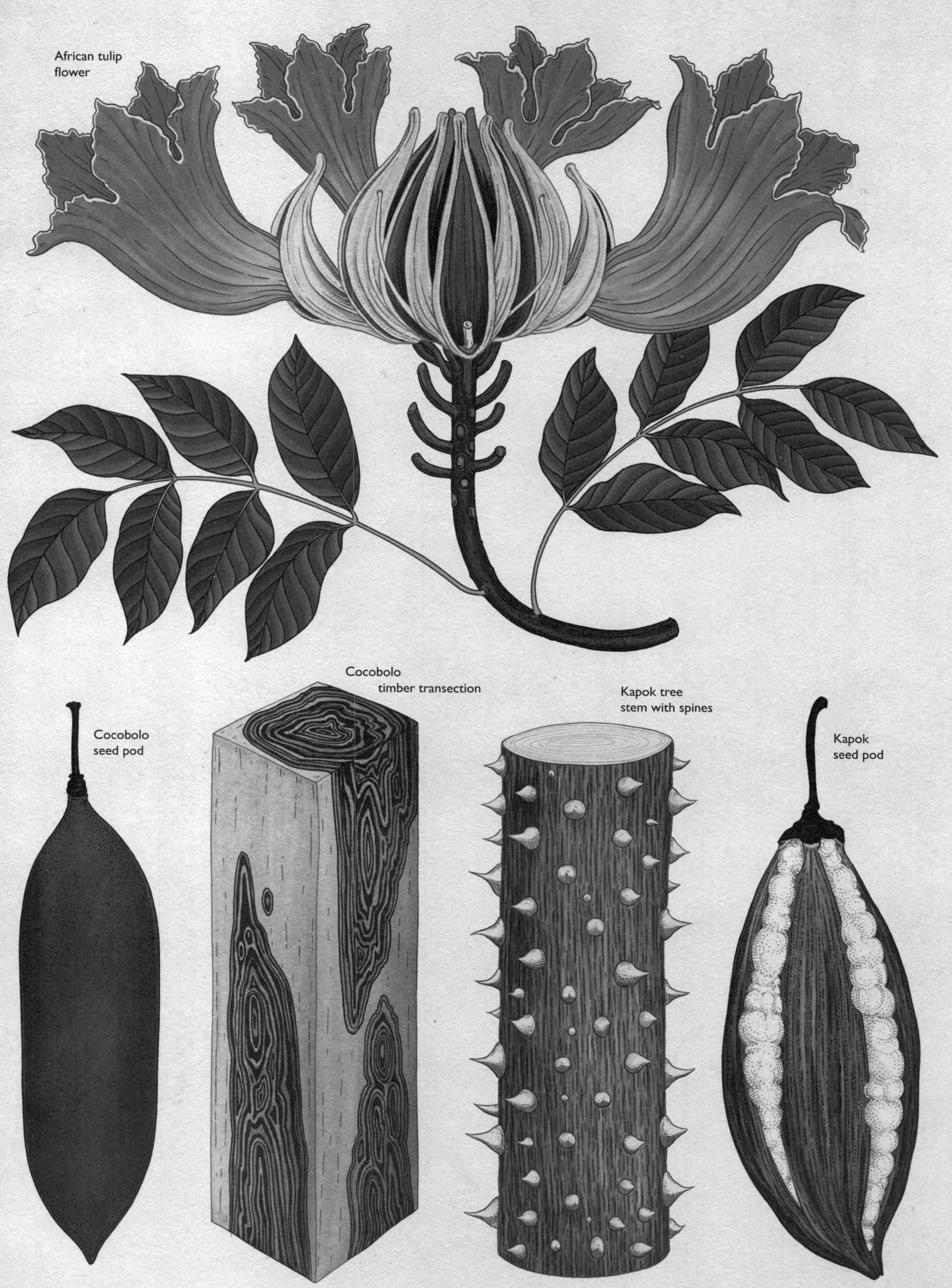

- Flame tree flower
- Flame tree leaf
- Fever tree flowers
- Whistling thorn leaves
- Frankincense cross section of trunk
- Frankincense resin
- Whistling thorn swollen thorn
- Fever tree leaves

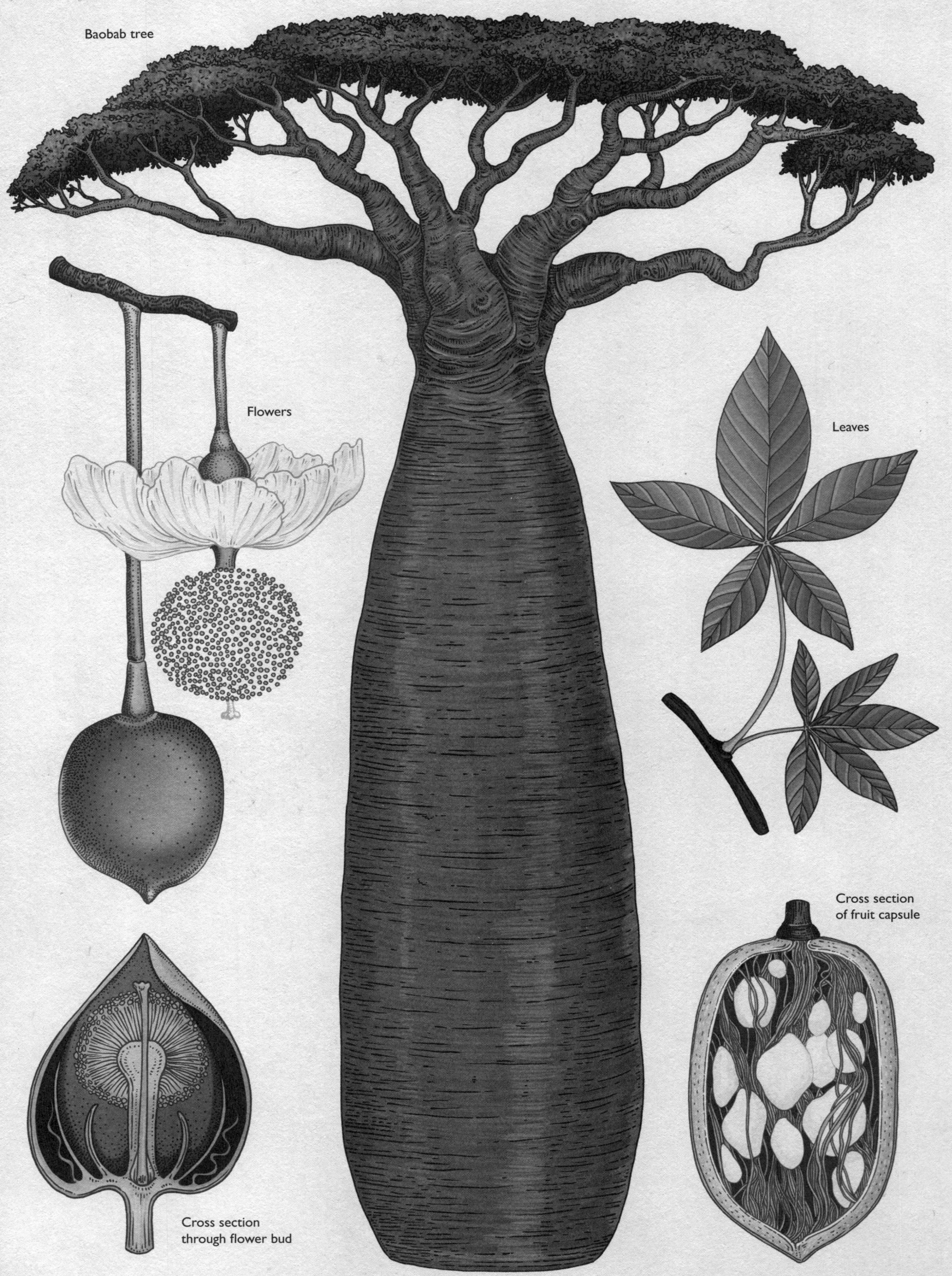

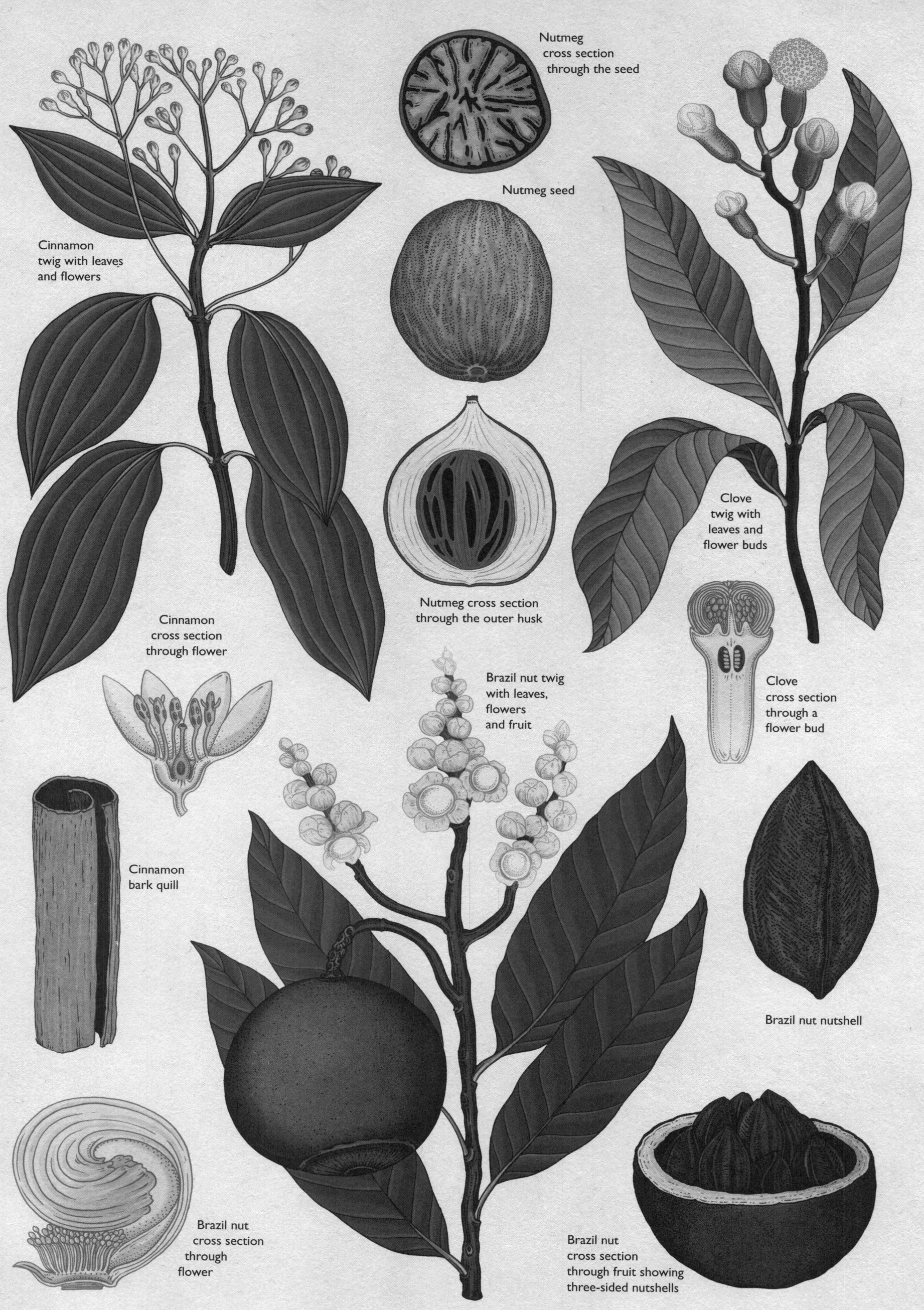

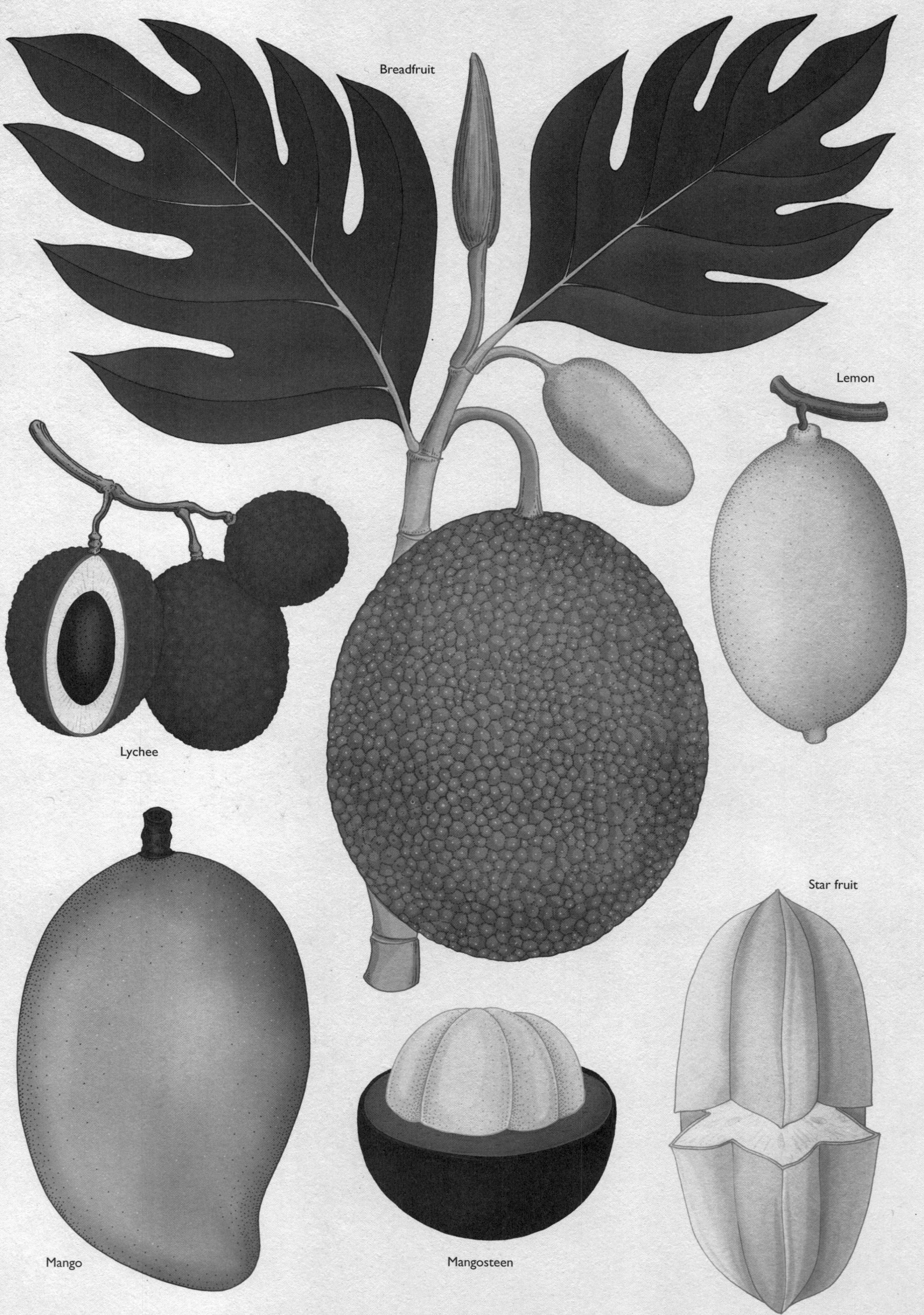

Yoshino cherry Contorted willow Flowering crab apple